the moon with mars in her arms

Poetry Books By Carolyn Zonailo

The Wide Arable Land (1981)
A Portrait of Paradise (1983)
Compendium (1985)
Zen Forest (1987)
The Taste of Giving: New & Selected Poems (1990)
Nature's Grace (1993)
Memory House (1995)
Wading the Trout River (1997)
The Goddess in the Garden (2002)
The Holy Hours (2004)

the moon with mars in her arms

Carolyn Zonailo

Ekstasis Editions

Library and Archives Canada Cataloguing in Publication

Zonailo, Carolyn
    The moon with mars in her arms / Carolyn Zonailo.

Poems.
ISBN 1-894800-82-6

    I. Title.

PS8599.O63M66 2006   C811'.54   C2006-907119-2

Front cover art:"Moon Shadow"
Monoprint by Ottilie Douglas
Back cover art: Portrait of CZ, Old Port Montreal, 2005
Charcoal drawing by Monique Patenaude

The author wishes to thank Stephen Morrissey for love and suppport;
Richard Olafson of Ekstasis Editions for his dedication to poetry and
literary publishing; Jeff Simpson for encouragement; Sandra
Richmond for sharing her ideas; Jean Shepherd for editorial assis-
tance; and Susan Ward for her invaluable inspiration.

Published in 2006 by:
Ekstasis Editions Canada Ltd.   Ekstasis Editions
Box 8474, Main Postal Outlet   Box 571
Victoria, B.C. V8W 3S1   Banff, Alberta TOL OCO

THE CANADA COUNCIL | LE CONSEIL DES ARTS
FOR THE ARTS | DU CANADA
SINCE 1957 | DEPUIS 1957

BRITISH
COLUMBIA
ARTS COUNCIL
Supported by the Province of British Columbia

the moon with mars in her arms has been published with the assistance of
grants from the Canada Council for the Arts and the British Columbia Arts
Council administered by the Cultural Services Branch of the Government of
British Columbia.

Contents

blessing

*This book is dedicated
to Sascha and Matheo
with welcome and love.*

When a man wanted to play a trick on a buddy, he would take his knife and put it on the windowsill in the light of the full moon. In the morning the blade would be dulled and useless until re-sharpened. That stuck in my mind, because in astrology the Moon and Mars (knives) are inimical, or rather incompatible....

Alice O. Howell, *Jungian Symbolism in Astrology*

...the moon has not only a male manifestation as the centre of the spiritual world of matriarchal consciousness; it has also a feminine manifestation as the highest form of the feminine spirit-self, as Sophia, as wisdom. It is a wisdom relating to the indissoluble and paradoxical unity of life and death, of nature and spirit, to the laws of time and faith, of growth, of death and death's overcoming...it is a wisdom that is bound and stays bound to the earth, to organic growth, and to ancestral experience. It is the wisdom of the unconscious, of the instincts, of life and of relationship.

Erich Neumann, "On the Moon and Matriarchal Consciousness"

To begin to see through the eyes of the feminine soul, look at the appearance of things in moonlight compared to the light of the sun. The clarity, distinctness and certainty of daylight consciousness is replaced by a softer, more mysterious vision, the night peopled by beings invisible during the clear light of day. Then, too, sometimes the moon is totally dark. The brightest moonlight tonight will shortly become perfect darkness. In the dark of the moon, when only stars are visible, you can sometimes see miraculous things in the heavens....

Janet O. Dallett, *When the Spirits Come Back*

exile

My Body Is Also A Map

The first time I almost left my body
I went quietly. You dropped me
at the hospital ER
and drove to the airport
to catch a plane.
It happened so quickly
I forgot to cry out loud or protest.
There were no angels hovering.
Later on, during the week it took
for my lungs to expel stale air,
unbidden messages came to me
at unexpected times, in various ways.
Once I was standing
on the Métro platform, people
all around, the loud roar
of the train entering the station
when suddenly a voice spoke.
And still later, when I was walking
uphill in pale, spring sunshine,
forcing myself to breathe and walk,
again a voice assailed me.
I got used to hearing messages,
prayers, whispers of mortality.
I even learned to breathe again
and gradually lost the sensation
of being underwater and drowning.
I came back to live in the climate and air
humans have long since adapted to.

I began to understand the map
my body had become—this road
leading to a known destination

or a secret passage of the heart;
another artery leading out toward
the cosmos, immortality, and the limits
of knowledge. After all, the body
is where we live. It can be read
like the palm of one's hand
when placed face up
in front of a skilled practitioner.

The second time I was even more
nonchalant, doing the dishes
en route to the emergency room,
taking time to organize household chores
on my way to the other world.
Curious how calmly it happened,
like a camera running everything
in slow motion, each gesture distinct.
There were no voices, messages, glimpses
of heaven or hell—in fact the whole thing
as if another one of life's daily tasks—
straightening up, I'll be back soon,
tonight's dinner is in the fridge.
The road map of my body leading
to the common place, the everyday,
the quotidian feat of staying
incarnated. As if it's all that simple,
the internal compass pointed "to life"
rather than "to spirit." And then
a slow recovery, no messages to guide me
as the known was definitely left behind,
the map a crisscrossing of valleys,
mountain peaks, unnamed rivers,
the everyday become a wilderness.

This is the first poem
I have written since then,
when the map veered off

into unknown territory,
the sheer sides of mountains
sheets of rock, the valleys green
and lush beyond springtime,
the river a dazzling golden colour.
Here is a poetic utterance
spoken like a primal scream
from a poet who lives in a place of exile,
in a body that is also a map.

My Body Is A Machine

My body is a machine
but there is no warranty,
few spare parts
and no guaranteed life span.
"Why do they call it
the golden years?"
I overhear one elderly woman
say to another; and then,
"The body is a machine,
the doctor diagnosed ageing."

The physiotherapist tells me
athletes fine-tune their bodies,
getting more performance
by pushing beyond pain
and limits of normal endurance.

I am endeavouring
to live with and in my body,
trying to make peace
with how my body
changes from this to that
without warning.
Entering the donut
of the MRI machine
I hear a strange music,
the metallic clink
as a magnetic field
images my vertebrae.

Am I the eye inside
these five senses: seeing,
tasting, smelling—
or the I that drives
the machine?
Am I a consciousness,
a brain sitting on top
of the corporeal me?

I have wanted to give up
this poem, as it becomes
one unbroken, unanswered
question mark,
slipping from the page
and from my mind
but when I turned on the TV
there it was again,
one character saying to another
"your body is just a machine"
so that everywhere I hear
this phrase as if it were
a known and accepted fact—
no philosophical debate,
further speculation,
or religious doctrine necessary—
just mechanical principles
and Darwinian theory.

A cousin received a transplant
heart; he made it through
the months of trauma and sickness
so that now the new heart
beats within his chest.

His wife of over thirty years
says her mild-mannered husband
is different: he bangs his hand
upon the table beside the dinner plate—
aggressive, angry, demanding—
not at all like the man she has loved;
she says they never argued
during all their married years.

"Cellular memory" the author of
The Heart's Code calls it,
challenging our idea
that the heart is just
a marvelous mechanical pump
and not an organ of memory and soul.
Imagine: someone else's self
could accompany the transplant
heart, a personality ingrained
upon the organ, what the author
describes as "soul stuff" imprinted
in the mechanical body.

Piecing together the fragments
of this poem, I return to its
beginning, a circle of question,
inked pages falling away,
thoughts suspended into sleep,
the phrase running beside me
as I hum along inside my body.

Flesh Falls Away

For Jackie, 1969-2001

At the end, our loved ones
disappear as we try to hold them
in the world our arms
can encompass;
but the flesh falls away,
the body becomes "rag"
and "bone"
skin so transparent
bones pierce through
at the hip, bleeding
all life from the sick,
the dying.

Soft contours of buttocks,
breast; muscle of thigh;
roundness of arms;
beauty of face—
fading into memory.
Finally the skeleton emerges,
the visible power of bones
a sculpted architecture.

Helpless, we watch the body
no longer a container
but an outgrown carapace,
shed skin of snake,
spiraled shell of nautilus.
And a quiet no voice
can speak across,
a silence as spirit
slips through bone, skin, flesh.

Left behind the vulnerable body,
the insistence of touch.
She who lived in beauty
and brightened our hearts
now lives as light itself:
Goodbye, we loved you.

   Hello, you live inside us now.

When I Die

*Mirrors are doors through which Death
comes and goes. Don't tell anyone. Besides,
look at yourself all your life in a mirror and
you will see Death at work like bees in a glass
hive.*
—Jean Cocteau

Now and then I catch
a glimpse of my younger
selves; passing a mirror
I wonder, "Who is this?"
Always making adjustments,
lowering expectations,
making new discoveries.

Years ago the irrevocable differences
were revealed to me:
young versus old;
healthy versus sick;
wealthy versus poor.
The rich know nothing
about the working life
of poverty and want.
The healthy do not understand
how to cope with illness.
And the young have no idea
of the future, the inevitable
goal of becoming elderly.

When I die, I will leave
my body, become ether
or spirit or nothingness;
pass on from this earthly home

to the realm of souls,
perhaps to gaze upon Divine
Light or enter an eternity
of darkness or be carried
forward on the wheel
of reincarnation, returned
to earth once more. But
nevertheless, leaving behind
this shelter where
I have been used to living.
When I was young, I feared
mortality—a strange child,
even then concerned
with time and the linear
passage of days, weeks, months.
In fact, I remember always
being conscious of the clock,
the circle of day to night,
cycle of season to season.

From my first breath
I began dying:
a race against time.
When I die please place
my body in the ground,
where grass can grow
above it, birds circle
overhead, and clouds
gather on the horizon.
On the stone
that marks my grave
carve name and epitaph,
add the dates of birth
and death—
then identify my craft:
POET.

In this way—
poem after poem—I have
measured the time I spent
in my body, recording
the poems that arrived,
insistent to be heard—by me,
if not by anyone else.
Each separate poem
an entire cosmos: in writing
I become every poet
who has ever lived.
I become the first poem I read—
an insignificant rhyme—yet
still remembered decades later.

In its entirety my poetry
aimed for peace, for love,
forgiveness and for truth.
Beauty—if achieved at all—
was purely a gift,
nothing of my invention.

I doubt that I will go
out singing and perhaps
not even in prayer—
but I hope at least
to say thank you to my body
for giving me a home
while here on earth;
and to the muse of poetry,
for filling my life
with moments when it seemed
time could stop, to allow
a thing observed or a feeling
felt to intensify and condense.

Poetry moved me further
into a consciousness
of intimate detail
or lyric moment—those
instances of *poiesis,*
of making or composition
that became my poems.

Last Will And Testament

I give my soul to God.
I give my body to the earth.
I give my poems to posterity.
I give my spirit to tolerance.
I give my mind to the future.
I give my thoughts to scholars.
I give my sex life to biographers.
I give my dreams back to the collective.
I give my smile to the lonely.
I give my e-mails to cyberspace.
I give my wisdom to the stars.
I give my confessions to the ocean.
I give my childhood to an orphan in Africa.
I give my vote to citizens in a totalitarian state.
I give my freedom of speech to a fundamentalist.
I give the words, *Life is to create*, to my tombstone.
I give my hope to the next generation.
I give my ideals to the unborn.
I return the life stories to friends who shared with me.
I leave my heart to those I love.

Living In Exile

But we were wrong and the map was true
and had we stood and looked about
from our height of land, we'd have had a view
which, since, we have had to learn by heart.
      —P.K. Page, "The Map"

We are living in exile, the snow deep
and icicles like swords of barbarians,
frost covering the window, intricate lace,
the air so cold it burns my lungs
cutting deep into airways too sensitive
to breathe in this frozen land. Through
weeks of winter we have lost our bearings,
the compass needle set to a northern point,
the afternoon sky already turning away from blue—
but we were wrong and the map was true.

This is the exact spot we were meant
to inhabit, arriving—despite the blinding storm—
at this place, to call this home, forgetting
where we came from or want to travel to.
It is here and only here, at half past midnight
when it is below minus twenty degrees out
and the fields sleep under their blanket of snow,
the dairy cows housed in their barns, walls cracking
with frozen night sounds, minds resting from doubt.
And had we stood and looked about

the land as it lay around our white, wooden
farmhouse, circa 1880, in the darkness
of this January night, the sky so clear with stars,
everything frozen and still and silhouetted
under the light of a full moon shining,
the snow glistening, the sparks that flew
from our wood stove briefly suspended in the air
as if brightly frozen—we would have held
each other in a warm embrace and felt new.
From our height of land, we'd have had a view

of the Trout River, a layer of snow over ice
with footprints down the middle of the river
where we had walked earlier in the daylight.
Living in exile, we have made love in the heat
of summer, in this same slow, shallow river.
We thought we longed to stay, as in the start,
in bodies that would be forever young, in seasons
that were not winter, in places that were
not exile, but homes created by family and art,
which, since, we have had to learn by heart.

—Huntingdon, Quebec
1992-1997

The Garden Of The Dead*

Spring is late coming, bleeding hearts
and bachelor buttons, rain on the scented lilacs.
Here are the iris—small, intensely blue,
the bearded yellow iris, lavender ones,
some a pale rust or cinnamon colour.
In a garden near the park, deep purple iris
unfurl from their pointed bud,
so dark they are almost black.

I've never seen this colour iris, solemnly
tinged like the Queen of the Night tulip.
Large, showy petals drape dramatically
as if sheer fabric. They are stately,
somber, funereal—this dark clump
among the lively hued flowers.

I have often written about
the miracle of spring returning—
first tender shoots of saffron crocus,
the perfect white camellia;
poems that celebrate Eve and her many gardens
full of flowers, fruit, abundance—
giant zinnias so colourful as if cut
from children's construction paper.

But now my poem is an elegy
for the harvest of the dead;
an offering for those who feel loss
and who will continue to grieve;

a tribute for those who kept their courage alive
when they became a grisly kind of gardener
as they dug, ploughed, and raked
through the garden of the dead:
not empty, but filled with memory,
with literal pieces of each individual's life.

This garden is planted with parts of corpses,
planted with fear and panic and tears,
planted with the seeds of war—
and now, as poet, I write
my poem about a garden
unlike all the other Edens of growth.
May the garden of the dead
grow tolerance and peace,
grow wisdom and learning,
grow love and healing
in this new century.

It has been a late spring,
unusually cold—it was difficult
to force the new growth forward
but trees have fresh, mint-coloured leaves,
flowers are unfolding, deep purple iris
among the yellow and blue and lavender ones.

* "And the cleanup of the World Trade Center remains has reached completion. A worker whose job entailed raking the fields of debris looking for human remains, described his function in an NPR interview as, 'a gardener gardening in the garden of the dead'."

Burqa

At last, the perfect outfit,
the one all women
have been waiting for
and centuries of couturiers
have strived to envision:
the ultimate female attire.

Herstory can be followed
through all cultures and ages
viewing the clothes
that women have worn:
feet bound into tiny sizes,
a wasp-like waist,
a nun's surplice,
the sensual sari,
whale-bone corset,
hoop skirt,
flapper dress,
a power suit,
flowered housedress,
off-the-shoulder ball gown,
bosom-flattering empire,
Victorian petticoats—
the human mind has designed
an almost endless parade
of fashion shape and form
to fit, conceal, adorn,
accentuate, sculpt
and present the soft shape
of a woman's body—
breast and buttock,
hips and waist,
neckline and thighs,
the ankle, the foot,

the throat and curve of spine,
backless, strapless, topless,
form-fitting, A-line—
we have pretty much
run the gamut.

Until now, in the beginning
of the twenty-first century,
a singular tradition made universal:
cover the female body
from crown of head
to tip of foot
in an all-encompassing tent:
not even the face revealed.

Here is the answer
to every clothes dilemma
the fair sex has ever deliberated.
Simply make the woman invisible.
She will see no evil
hear no evil
and especially speak no evil.
Woman will not tempt
man—drawing him
into the lure of female beauty.

Covered from top to bottom,
young women, old women—
no one can distinguish
age or intelligence,
class or race,
comely from plain,
svelte or curvaceous.

A few bright colours
or somber ones,
a swaddling of fabric
and presto—an entire
documentary of style
and human history
via the feminine
neatly sewn up,
under the wrap of the burqa.

Embrace the future,
let fabrication cease to exist,
let profit end,
let all women wear
the same outfit.

The mothers, daughters, wives
sisters, lovers,
the goddess in her many guises
will walk imperceptibly
throughout the world.

The early morning breeze
will stir the folds
of her coloured robe,
her loveliness seen by no one:
her eyes—those windows of the soul—
perfectly and forever concealed.

When all women wear burqas
it will be an amazing sight:
nothing left to be seen of a woman's body;
the decorative feminine,
the seductress,

the allure of being female
become a flowing cloth.
Here, in the twenty-first century,
fifty-two percent of human beings
will move silently, invisibly,
and oh, so gently,
slipping through the shadows
of a world where gender
is more powerful
than flowers or weapons,
than nations or culture,
than desire or imagination.

Beloved

We pray for peace in the world.
We pray for Mars and Venus to conjoin
　　in love, not war.
We pray for suicide bombers to choose
　　life over heaven.
We pray for peace marchers to have love
　　in their hearts, not hatred.
We pray for children to have food in their stomachs,
　　not empty bellies.
We pray for money to buy drugs to treat leprosy.
We pray for those who research a cure for AIDS.
We pray for the emerald mountains of Columbia
　　　that the farmers who live in those green
　　　valleys may live there in peace.
We pray for God to save Allah and Allah to save
Buddha and Buddha to save Shiva and Shiva
　　　to save the Virgin Mary, mother of us all.
We pray for the eternal soul of the *anima mundi.*
We pray, beloved, for spirit.
We pray the earth's prayer: that the silent ground
　　become sacred.
We pray for surrender of all weapons of mass destruction.
We pray for surrender in the arms of our beloved.
We pray for heaven on earth—now, not later.
We pray for peace, not revenge.
We pray to live without violence, because *the suffering
　　of a single child* is not worth all the world's religions.
We pray for a full harvest, we pray for rain,
　　for summer, spring and fall.
We pray for an end to nuclear weapons, biochemical weapons,
　　and to all other kinds of weaponry.
We pray for the newborn baby to find comfort.
We pray, beloved, for a peaceful end to all wars.
We pray for this prayer of peace to be heard by the people

of this earth.
We pray, beloved.
We pray to the Christians and Jews and Muslims and Hindus
and Buddhists and Sikhs and Taoists and Confucians
for an end to conflict.
We pray: do nothing. We pray: kill nobody.
We pray: sacrifice not even a single child in the name.
Beloved.

Name Change

"These youth love death as you love life."
—Osama bin Laden, 1996

At the beginning
it was a sense of awe
at the individual's action:
a hero, perhaps,
to give up their own life
for—what? political gain,
religious devotion, duty,
history—the glory
of an afterlife? Certainly
the emphasis was on *suicide,*
a voluntary giving up of body
and soul, to a cause
(supposedly) beyond the single
life, the unique fingerprint
of someone's existence
here on planet earth.

Now, as the deaths grow
in number, innocent persons
blown to pieces, injured
people suffering, sirens
and rubble in country
after country, victims carried
away on stretchers, blood
on city streets, in places
of worship or shopping or transport,
hotels or nightclubs, airplanes—

as time goes on, the emphasis
shifts to *bomber*,
an operative meant
solely to blow up, blast
apart, detonate and destroy.

Finally there has come
to be a change of name—
homicide bomber, the hero
become a murderer,
the physical body
no longer flesh, bone, spirit
but now a form of arms,
an object designed
to inflict bodily harm;
"the beauty of weapons"
no longer a metaphor
but a deadly reality:
the radiance of a unique soul,
no longer human, but weaponry,
to murder, maim and kill.

desire

I Have Carrried The World On My Shoulders

Go only as far in your mind
as your feet will carry you.

Do one thing at a time.
Don't try to do it well,
        just do it as best as possible.

Let cars drive fast;
ride the bus
and look out the window.

Take a breath in,
breathe out with an audible
sigh . . .in . . .sigh . . .in . . .sigh.

Wear red shoes on your feet
and walk along the boulevard
at a leisurely pace, slowly
putting one foot forward,
a step at a time.

Look skyward—see blue
skies, with puffy cumulus clouds
or thin cirrus ones overhead.

Buy a baseball cap
and wear sunglasses,
roll up shirtsleeves,
undo the top buttons.

Count the flowers: forsythia,
daffodils, hyacinth, tulips,
bleeding heart. Wait for lilacs
to scent the yards
and the bearded iris to unfurl.

Watch the trees begin to leaf—
weeping willow branches
turn a fresh green
before the leaves appear.

Slow everything down:
a day, the season of spring,
even your lifetime.

Put down all burdens,
lift the world from your shoulders.
Breathe in, ah, oh, O.

Imagine a world
where each one of us—
you, me—we are all alive
in this single moment,
slow as a breath
exhaling in a long sigh.

Oh, the birds...

Oh, the birds have returned
to our neighbourhood
after a long winter,
coldest one on record
for sixty years.

The raucous, cheeky song
of the bright cardinal
whistles from the tops of trees;
a red flash as he flies
from one yard to another.

Sparrows twitter and cheep
as they come and go,
rebuilding their nest
in the space between the eaves,
getting ready to hatch offspring.

Now they fluff their feathers
to keep warm, appear
twice their normal size;
mate under the cover
of the front porch,
a dance of wings and chatter,
part of their seasonal celebration.

Grackles have arrived
filling the apple tree
for a brief time
large and noisy birds
here, then on their way again.

Soon the yellow finches
will fly over the flowers,
hummingbirds will hover
at the next-door feeders,
and, at 5 p.m., butterflies
will land on my pink dress;
the sparkle of fireflies
on a hot summer night.

And, sometimes, the flash of blue
as a jay flies by,
that glorious, marvelous
bit of sky come down
to live at eye-level—
while the gentle sigh
of the mourning dove
coos and calls
from the tree turned green.

Those first few days
of soft, barely-there colour
before the leaves open—
so much promise
in that almost-hue—
come to full potential
when the turtle doves sing.

The ever-cheerful robin
replaces winter chickadees
as the common bird
most easily identified.
Red-winged blackbirds,
elegant and dapper,
display a fanfare of scarlet
as they take flight.

Down the street, seagulls
scavenge at the corner store
dumpster, land-locked but bold.
Pigeons land on balconies,
not frightened by the plastic owl
placed there to discourage
their nesting and mewing.

The trickster crow hops here
and there, black as midnight;
a murder of crows gathered
in the yard, a friend says,
the day they brought her home,
newly born, omen of her life
to unfold in the decades to come.

Oh, the birds fall
from the sky, they fly
and dive and peck and sing
and sleep among the branches;
bird-song starts in pre-dawn
full throttle by waking time.

They fly by mistake
into plate glass doors,
crash against the windows
of skyscrapers downtown,
bless our avenues
and boulevards and streets
and homes and balconies,
parks, yards, gardens
with colours, song and soul.

Oh, the birds....

Afternoon Sleep

I want a perfect body,
no aches, no pain, free
from any blemish, not even
a bruise or miniscule cut,
not a hangnail or a small mole.

I want another's body
to lay down beside
my perfect body
on blue cotton sheets
that are soft and freshly
laundered, with pillows plumped
and an overhead fan
slowly turning, a cooling
breeze drifting
over our bodies
on a summer afternoon.

No movement, just a fan
as it circles above us;
no touch, two bodies
breathing in unison;
the fan stirring the air,
breathing in/out,
as we lie asleep together,
each of us in our own dream.

Complete freedom from care,
suspended in the collective unconscious
without so much as a memory.

Learning To Float

ONE

I remember falling back
onto the water
as if lying upon a mattress,
my feelings a mix
of fear and pleasure,

someone to place their hands:
one under my head, cupping it;
the other at the base of my neck
to keep my face from sinking
under the water—

and then, star-fishing my arms and legs
away from my sides,
slightly arching my back
to tilt my head lower

as the hands were removed
and I sank slowly down into the water
like snuggling into a down comforter

mouth and nose still
above, in the breathable air,
my limbs held motionless,
face looking upward
to the clouds and blue sky.

There I was—floating
eyes-up in the ocean pool,
only the water holding
my body buoyant.

Later, I learn to extend
the floating time
by gently moving my arms,
paddling just a bit
with my hands to stay afloat.

Ah, what a joy it was
to be a child,
to grow up beside the ocean
and to float in the salt water.

TWO

Salt water makes it easier
to float, the body
more buoyant in saline waters,
like a natal womb
suspended in the cosmic sea.
Our lungs develop, grow
ready to inhale oxygen—

that first gasp of air, then
exhalation, the urgent
cry of a baby during C-section,
loud exclamation of sound
before being lifted free.

The newborn's howl announces
birth—like arriving at a shoreline,
washed up into another
incarnation: I am, I am.

This initial outcry
a salutation of confidence—
that someone will hear
and comfort, hold and wash clean,
feed and maintain.

And so we are held
in loving arms,
nursed by mothers and fathers,
nurtured into infancy, then
childhood, then adult life
and finally death—
the body placed in earth,
the soul returning to ether.

We can float, only temporarily,
in the salt water of a seaside beach—
lying face up toward
a bright, blue sky—
for this instant of childhood,
taking an extraordinary delight
in the sensation of having learned to float.

THREE

A star, the basic
back float is called
une étoile sur le dos.

Yes, a star on your back,
five-pointed like da Vinci's
drawing—flung-out arms,
extended legs, head on top

to form a pentagram,
mystic symbol of male
and female in balance;

the image of perfection,
Blazing Star of mystery
and synthesis.

As you assume this pose
open yourself
like a rose bud
blooms in summer sun
to become full-blown.

Rest upon salt water
like nestling into freshly
fallen snow

spread your limbs
as if about to make
a snow angel

then, hold that position—
that moment of openness,
that motion of almost,

let the star on your back
radiate through the universe

so these minutes
of conscious suspension

can be remembered—years
and even decades later—

a scene from your childhood
when you floated freely

ah, held there
on the sea of life.

Dead Man's Float

ONE

Don't be afraid to let go
of the known. Take a deep
breath and remember: you

won't be able to breathe
under the water. The trick
is to give up, go limp, surrender

and launch yourself face first
into the liquid element—your body
horizontal, your limbs hanging

down, dangling from the trunk,
loose like a jelly-fish, a feeling
of being gelatinous, without substance.

Then you become a floating object,
not a stone that sinks or anchor
that reaches down to find a fastening

but a composition like pumice
or styrofoam, a bottle with secret message
bobbing on the surface of the ocean.

This way, you experience *the incredible
lightness of being*, as if not needing air,
temporarily free from the necessities

of living on land. You can open
your eyes to see underwater. There
are schools of needlefish near you.

Then, the sudden need to breathe
again, to return to friends, the beach,
and a hot sun shining over you.

TWO

Just let go: fall
face first into the clear
lake water. Surrender.
Let your limbs go limp,
arms falling below your body,
legs hanging down,
your back slumped over
like a dead person.

You can open your eyes
to see the mud bottom,
lake reeds under you,
and the miracle of minnows
swimming around your body.

Someone on the shore—your father—
is calling, telling you
not to put your face in the water;
come home, return to camp,
to his protection, to where other children
are playing at the edge of the water.

Resurrect from this willing
suspension, this forward
tilt away from life
into the lake's black depth,
with the smell of woods in it,
and an underlife of tiny fish
you can observe from this position—
so fascinating to see below
the surface, in such clear detail,
you want to float forever.

THREE

Could be useful
in an emergency—
such as shipwreck—
to avoid drowning.

Assume the dead man's float;
go all over limp.
It conserves energy.

Just lift the mouth and nose
occasionally above water level,
to exhale and inhale.

Otherwise, suspend yourself,
hang in there, using
your own body
as a lifesaver.

Swimming—unless the shore
is within sight—takes up
too much strength.
Wait, in this frontal slump
to be rescued.

The poetics of space;
The psychoanalysis of fire;
On poetic imagination and reverie;
Water and dreams.

Sunset Over Côte St. Luc Shopping Centre

After a blue sky day
a few wispy clouds drift
across the setting sun;
at the bottom of our street
the shopping centre provides
a skyline for the golden glow;
as the sun begins to set
the sky beams with colour—
first going bright with yellow hue
then softening into pink tones
above the grocery store, the pharmacy
and Blockbuster Video. I've watched
the sun set behind rolling mountains,
its beauty reflected on the surface
of a nestled lake; the bountiful
calm of sunset seen twice over,
imaged in the watery mirror.

I've followed the orb of sun
as it sank into the Pacific Ocean,
horizon dotted with western islands,
the entire sky lit up with orange
and gold and yellow—colours lingering
long after the sun has set.
And then the final rosy blush
to echo the maritime refrain:
red sky at night, brings sailor's delight....

Above the Côte St. Luc Shopping Centre
this spectacle of nature is more
mundane, the backdrop of commerce,
daily shopping and parking lot,
utilitarian in design and function.

And yet, after the heat of a summer's day,
this miracle: all the glory
of sunsets I've viewed in scenic
landscapes recreated in the sky
above the IGA and Rona Hardware.
This benediction of light
offers both pleasure and beauty,
making a pause in the cycle
of day to evening to night,
while the sun sets in splendour
over Côte St. Luc Shopping Centre.

Sunset Over Lac St. Louis

"To the lighthouse!"
we call out to each other,
then laugh about the literary allusion,
talk about making out in the new car,
steaming up the windows—
you know, like teenagers
used to do, sit in cars
parked near any kind of beach
to kiss, fondle, grope
our way toward adult life.

We were in such a rush back
then, to grow up, leave home,
experience the act of going all the way,
everything a mystery it seemed.

Now sex often begins by age fourteen,
sex sells products, makes porn movies,
traverses gender lines—is anything
but mysterious. Really, we've come
here to park beside the lake
and stare out at the sunset
from this vantage point in Lachine,
a suburb of Montreal, named after China
and the Northwest Passage—leading,
they thought in those days, to spices
and the Orient, not furs and the Pacific.

The famous seaway was built to widen
and deepen the St. Lawrence River,
flooding villages so ships could pass
through from the Atlantic to the Great Lakes;
over a hundred and fifty years earlier,
a canal was constructed to circumvent
the rapids at Lachine. Here, at the lighthouse,
where the river opens into Lac St. Louis:
it's all there, recorded and available
to peruse at the Fur Trade Museum
in this lakeside town, beaches that
used to be for swimming, polluted now—
so we park at the lake's edge, to watch
the wind move across water.

Lac St. Louis widens out in waves
as the sun sets over Ste. Anne de Bellevue
and the sky is lit up with gold
that bounces off the water, the landscape
truly all a "shimmer", the sunset
long and lingering, like the tingle
of desire, the thrill of what
was unknown back in high school.

It was all yet to be known—
marriage, children, divorce,
falling in love all over again,
the intricate complexities of life
in the twenty-first century.

Now in the middle of our fifth
decade, the mystery is about time
remaining, the journey to old age
and beyond—whereas sex—
it still is sometimes a surprise,
when our tongues enter—ah,
forbidden zones—with excitement,
passion. Every age grows up,
fails to discover China, yet sails
out to find what they never
even dreamed would lie ahead.

I Have Listened To The World Sing

Sometimes it is a loud wail
of grief—anguish, fear, terror
pulling the world apart,
like ripping down the length
of a white cotton bed sheet
to use as blood-soaked bandages
as if the great cities themselves
knelt down, let tears stream
in mourning as their citizens died
bloody and violent and painful
deaths—all because of murderous
intent to kill the innocent.

At other times, it is the moans
pleasure brings, the sound of waves
across a pebble shoreline;
then the world sighs softly,
as moonlight shines with mystery
over the mirror-like surface of a lake
reflecting the muted shadows
of trees along the water's edge;
sounds like love-birds cooing
or naked lovers holding one another
while the open curtain lets light
from a full moon illuminate
shoulder, line of back, thighs.

I have heard the world laugh
with joy, cry with delight,
sing loudly—as if all peoples
were like one blessed family,
joining together everywhere

to express happiness—what
an amazing sound: love bursting
from everyone's hearts, the world
singing, "Praise! Praise!"

Oh, the world groans and cries
with the hunger of a child—
children begging with hands
outstretched, asking for mercy,
for charity, for help. And so I give
to a child ten thousand miles away
and keep her in my heart.
For the world's sake adopt
any child who needs your care
and the world will whisper, "thank you"
a sound like the wind in high cedars
or swaying through palm fronds;
a breeze blowing over the crest
of waves at sea, white foam flying
as a westerly brings fine weather.

Today I heard a dedicated man
play music from his childhood soul
and as he played, I could hear
the world pray quietly, each chord
of music brought grace a note
closer, opened hearts to meditate.
He took a lyric melody and played
it with a universal tune, so that
all who listen closely can hear
the world is patiently waiting
to let exquisite sounds of beauty
fill each day—for the world desires

pleasure, love, charity and laughter.
The world sings one person at a time;
a single note of music, a grateful moment
of peace—and then we all can listen
to the world sing: Om. Om. Om.

for the victims in London, a lament
for the music of Pat Metheny, merci
07/07/2005

blessing

Seed-Time: A Sonnet Sequence

Is There A Seed At The Center?

After they killed their father, the brothers
Hades, Zeus and Poseidon drew lots:
to Zeus, the heavens; to Poseidon, the seas;
to Hades, the underworld—doomed to dwell
alone in the deep and hidden recesses.

If it weren't for the pomegranate seeds, Demeter
would have kept her daughter, Persephone.
She, who was forced to live a shadow life,
could have returned to gather lilies and violets,
had she not eaten those potent, sweet seeds
to lodge her there in the kingdom of the dead.

At the center of every organism, it seems
a seed desires to grow—abundance dances
with decay—under, then up again, to re-seed.

The Kernel Of Age/ing

While Poseidon ruled over the oceans;
and Zeus shape-shifted to seduce;
Hades brooded, alone in his obscure kingdom.

And yet, what riches Hades owned—
the metals forged in the earth's core,
precious gemstones, and treasures
from the collective unconscious—these
belonged to the lord of the underworld.

Still, Hades felt the dread of his loneliness,
until the day he saw Demeter's daughter
carefree with her friends. Then Hades reaped
Persephone, plucked her as easily as picking
a flower, abducted her down to his dark
bed, where he fed her the seeds of his passion.

A Greening Season

Demeter went looking for her lost child;
the goddess of cereal, grain, the bread of life,
went weeping across the land, making
it barren, ruining the harvest. Finally

she appealed to Zeus—he said, the girl
could return to her mother, let the crops
grow again. If Persephone had not eaten
anything during her stay with Hades,
she could return to the meadows of her youth.

But Persephone had indeed bitten off
more than she could chew: the unsuspecting
bride, with her underworldly bridegroom
had tasted the fruit of their sexual union.
Did she eat the seeds in innocence, or intent?

Full-Blossoming

Persephone's return home brings the lands
back to growth and harvest and fruition.
These are planting seasons,
when the earth offers such variety
of flower, vegetable, fruit and grain.

But in the dormant season, Persephone leaves
to rejoin Hades. There, in the dark gloom
of their marriage bond, Persephone blossoms
to become King Death's own Queen, the prize

at the center of Hades' realm. His longing
and desire draws her down to him,
brings her back again and again,
the way a seed lies in moist earth,
holding within itself its own rebirth.

Wheel Of Life: Meditations

Our genetic code, contained in the molecules of DNA of each cell...is as different from other species as from each other. The individual and personal codes create each unique body shape and layout of organs. All this finely orchestrated complexity comes from one single fertilized egg cell, which holds half of our genetic code from our Mother, and the other half of the DNA from our Father's sperm.

Joyce Whitely Hawkes, Ph.D.

THE MOTHER PEARL @ THE WORLD'S CENTER

O Mother I love you.
I lay inside your womb,
and you carried me with you.
When you climbed the stairs
I ascended within you.

When your body rested
under warm blankets
and you curled into sleep
I swam inside you,
safe in my fetal position
like the edible flesh of a nut
hidden inside its hard shell.

A piece of grit in an oyster's
husk initiates layers of cushion
to form an opalescent pearl,
translucent, shining, round or
almost round, a white that
emanates subtle colours.

Mother is a pearl, the moon
a gigantic night-pearl
that changes shape during
the dark hours, from day
to day rounding out, then
waning down; suspended
from time for nine months.

O Mother, O pearl, O moon.

MOTHER EGG—SPLIT IN TWO PARTS

I slipped from the womb
like a shucked pea
from its pod—the green nest
split down the middle—

inside, sweet-tasting peas
lined up in a row,
delicate as a newborn's toes
and fingers, ripened perfectly

in mother's full belly.
The fertilized egg split
in two halves—from Father,
from Mother—a blueprint

for the future, to be divided
again: half to my son,
half to my daughter.

Then again, to my granddaughter,
the mother egg constantly
splitting into the next
set of perfect fingers,
tiny toes, peas all lined up

in a peapod, ready
to grow into this miracle,
the blessing of each life
as it emerges, surfaces,
draws breath as soul enters.

And, what do we know?
The night is long.
The day is short.
Shout for joy! Hello!

ALL THE EGGS YOU NEED FOR A LIFESTYLE/LIFETIME

My mother loved me in the womb
An unknown soul, male or female,
Not glimpsed by her, just naked
Soul to body, two in one.

If a girl, already bestowed
With all the eggs for her lifetime—
Or a lifestyle without offspring.
Every month, when ovulation occurs
An egg, ripe and ready, slips

Into eternity or down through a flood
Where the unfertilized egg is carried
Through blood, past its prime, then away.

Pieces That Fit Together

What if each individual soul
is completely unique—
maintains a soul print
carried with them *life*

after life, body after body,
their soul eternal—a concept
beyond the time and space
dimensions we live on earth.

Not to heaven nor to hell,
only to be reborn again,
the wheel of reincarnation,
but each time retaining
our own soul's DNA.

Tears Of Fire: Four Poems

A FLAME BURNS HOT & COOL

It feels like the forces of darkness
are hammering at the door—
conflict, division, brutality, destruction.

When evils were most free, bodies were piled
one on top of another on top of another;
the life literally gassed out of each person,
or starved until the body an emaciated
stick-like figure, nothing but bone covered
with *raggedy skin* and dumped into a pit.

She said, "He doesn't believe in the holocaust."

Can not believe.

Will not believe.

Does not believe.

Does not want to believe that over five million
people bathed in euphemistic showers;
baked in euphemistic ovens;
dug their own graves only days before dying.

A friend was married to a man
who was a survivor: he had a visible number
tattooed on his skin. One day I saw him
with another woman. After their divorce,
my friend married an opera singer
many years younger than her.
They returned to live in Germany
so that he could sing Wagner
in opera houses across Europe.

I fear the forces of darkness
are hammering at the door....

TEARS OF COMFORT, TEARS OF PAIN

Prayer to the west wind: let the soft
breeze of sleep bless me with dreams
that are vivid, full of details and colour.

Entreaty to the east: bring a strong scent
of cinnamon with a lilt of rose petal
into my bed chamber, sensuous and real.

Invocation to the northern gale: blow
with gusto and determination through every
season and fill me with the will to survive.

O spirit of the south, I beseech: when
I grow tired, help me to slumber in peace;
when I wake, open my mind to new hope.

With An Open Space

Bull's eye, or the margin around it.
A question mark.
Ideas: speculation?

The ten seconds of silence
before the long dash.

Together, each one
talking on their cell phone.

The space between youth
and old age.

Ground zero.

RATIONAL ANGER

Yellow, purple, lavender, vanilla,
russet, blue-coloured irises
in gardens up the hill
and down—miniature ones,
large, bearded varieties—
hued from rust to dusty brown;
golden sunshine to palest lemon;
robin's egg to midnight indigo.

This the flower Van Gogh painted
with energetic brush strokes
as if the flowers were in motion—
life force bursting from iris
to canvas to viewer—nothing tidy
about this flower that grows in a clump
of colour, with movement and vigour.

It was as if the *fleur de lis*
seared through his mind, stirred
his emotions to the point
of pure creativity: natural beauty
betrayed by his own incapacity
for tranquility or forgiveness.

The struggle between painting and object
seemed to change from passion
to anger and finally to rage
as he measured the distance
between his rendition and nature.

In a gesture of rational anger, he
sliced at his ear—although
beauty had entered through the eye—
it wasn't silence he needed
but blindness—where the blue
of iris, the blaze of sunflower
could not burn into his brain.

In the act of shooting himself,
he sought the darkness—
but when he lingered at the edge
of life, sight did not shut down
immediately: he complained
perfection was not possible
to attain, not even in death.

Halfmoon Of Solitude: Poem Cycle

ONE EYE ON EARTH & ONE EYE ON HEAVEN

In the beginning, Gaia gave
shape to herself, the Earth.
She then created her son and husband,
Ouranos, the Sky. They lay together,
two entities each as large as the other,
with Sky on top of Earth. And so they
were joined in perpetual embrace,
an ongoing, endless sexual union.
Ouranos, filled with lust for Gaia,
mated with her continuously. Earth
gave birth to sons and daughters, plus
other creatures whom Ouranos despised.
He stuffed them back into Earth's womb.

But their youngest son, Chronos,
was clever and spiteful. He hated
his lustful and eccentric father.
Chronos fed his loathing of the Sky
god, wanting to kill his father.

In violent action, Chronos sliced
off his father's genitals. Then Sky could
no longer mate with Earth. Ouranos
ascended to become the Heavens,
and Gaia, no longer joined in copulation,
became Mother Earth, finally able to release
her previously-conceived children.

Chronos flung his father's dismembered
sex organs into the ocean. Still potent,
they mixed with the sea foam;
out of this combination of spume
and the bloody genitals of Ouranos
Aphrodite, the goddess of love and beauty,
was born. She washed to shore
on a sea shell, beautiful to behold.

And so the prolonged act of love
between the Earth and the Sky
did indeed give birth to many beings,
and even as their mating ceased
when Ouranos was rendered impotent,
his genitals—when tossed away—
still had the power to create Aphrodite,
daughter of the Sky god Ouranos,
no mother to birth her shining beauty.

CLOUDS OF BECOMING

*There is another cosmogony, or account of the creation,
according to which Earth, Erebus and Love were the first
of beings. Love (Eros) issued from the egg of Night, which
floated on Chaos. By his arrows and torches he pierced and
vivified all things, producing life and joy.*

My father loved me when he
entered my mother. His passion
fertilized my conception.
It was love that drove him
to pursue desire.
Love engendered my birth.

I arrived into the world,
after a short labour
and only nine months' wait.
Eros was there, at my beginning,
when my parents made love together.
They wanted a girl child
to keep my brother company.

Yes, love forced me into being.
Love began my infant heart
beating each measurable pulse
so that my heart speaks
"love—love—love".
Nothing divine, except the spark
of God in me: my life
a mortal one, entirely human.

Nevertheless, it is love has led me
down each garden path;
love has whispered inspiration
into my inner ear, birthed each poem
I've written. Love conceived
both children that I bore;
love joined me in union
with every lover, husband, friend.

The only wisdom we need
is to know that love
makes the world go around.
Love sets our hearts in motion.
Love brings us into existence.
Here is a simple way to live—
decide that during your
indeterminate time
here upon earth—
make love your only mission.
Eros or *thanatos*. Take a stand
for love, as death
will come sooner or later
without any choice.

KEEPING AN EYE ON THE FULL MOON

Sometimes, when the moon is full,
we look together out the bedroom window
to see the full moon as it shines,

illuminating the yard with a soft glow:
moonlight shapes long shadows on snow
from the bare branches of the apple tree

or the amber globe of a harvest moon
playing hide and seek between
the full-leaved limbs of taller trees.

Always there is a mystery to this light
the full moon casts across the backyard
where it is usually dense with darkness at night.

But on these full moon evenings, everything
is visible, tinged with the sheen of a silver patina.
I often think of pirates or runaway lovers—

anyone who needs the cover of total obscurity,
unable to make their moves in secret or in stealth
when the full moon shines with her strange light.

This is not anything like sunshine,
the clear details of day's light,
but a nocturnal kind of visionary brightness—

yet, full so briefly, then the changing
shapes as the moon wanes, pares down,
prepares to fall into becoming invisible.

The Moon Eclipsing

Late at night, in warm or winter weather,
my love and I would often walk
the half mile of highway
and the other half mile
of side road, to reach the old bridge
that crossed over the Trout River.

From the crest of the wood-planked
bridge, we looked down to see
the river frozen enough to walk on
or flowing toward town in warmer seasons.

We would also look upward,
to view the night sky, where overhead
in the darkness of countryside
stars plentiful beyond our comprehension
were visible. We would point out major
constellations, sometimes see comets
or a shooting star....

One night, as we walked toward
the bridge, a full moon low to the horizon
slowly grew dark, as the black shade
of the earth drew across the moon,
eclipsing the moon's light. It was a cold
night and on that country side road
it seemed we were the only humans
alive. We could then imagine the great
power an eclipse of the moon
would have held for the primitive minds
of long-distant ancestors—without
electricity, cars, refrigerators, large
urban centers—to see the shadow cast by earth
as it crossed between sun and moon.

And to feel that humans, throughout history
had watched this same phenomenon—
in fear, in awe, in prognostication.
Despite the chilly temperatures, we lingered
as long as possible, to watch as
the eclipse overtook the moon. The drama
of this event remains still vivid,
years now since my love and I walked
that country road late at night, watching
moon and stars in all four seasons.

Now the elegant old bridge
has been torn down, replaced
by an inferior concrete one that lacks
all aesthetic and romance. We still
watch an eclipse when possible,
but confined to what can be seen
in our urban surroundings
where the sky is dimmed by city lights
and that intense feeling of seeing stars
or moon as if for the first time ever
can't be recaptured, except in memory.

Morrison Side Road
Huntingdon, Quebec
—1992-1997

New Hope: Poems

DOWN THE ROAD TO THE FUTURE—GOING FAST

The more we hang onto the past
    the faster we reach the future.
Times change, the world reshapes
    itself, cycles repeat:
        but new ideas also arrive.

Re:Vision—in order to see clearly
    You Must Revise Your Life.

Stafford woke up the morning of his death
    early, as usual, and composed in hand-writing
        what became his final poem
            before anyone else was awake.
        He also wrote a letter to a friend that day.
    An active man, he was aged 79, when he died.
Later, his family found the poem and letter in his study.

Hilde, my mentor, was a medium. She died in 1999, in her 90th
    year. Hilde lived in Germany during two world wars.
        She worked in the underground against the Nazis;
            when she was brought before the Gestapo
        her psychic powers saved her life.
    Near her death she warned me "If you want to travel
do it sooner than later. The worst is yet to come."

My ancestors were Doukhobors. They were *spirit wrestlers*
and pacifists. In Russia, during the nineteenth century,
no one could force them to kill a fellow human
not in the name of the Czar, nor in the name of their country,
not even in the name of God.

Peasants, they were willing to face torture to cling
to this original idea on their own: the year was 1895
when they burned their firearms and stood in front
of soldiers on horseback, unarmed.

Now we are going fast down the road—to the future.
Where the road forks, will we make a decision
to go this way, or the other?

Every Stripe A New Day

I'm not very young
But I'm not really old
I'm somewhere in the middle

Every day is a new day
And I live each one
A day at a time

Because I'm old enough
to know there's not all
That much I do know

But I think a lot
About the young
In one another's arms

How every time I hear
Someone say "There's
Nothing we can do"

A voice inside me disagrees
We are all—young and old—
In each other's arms

Like the rings in a tree's trunk
Or stones along a river bed
Or stars in heaven above

OUTGOING CIRCLES OF OPPORTUNITY

May and Mabel Moroso, sisters,
were my father's aunts. I knew
them as Auntie May and Aunt Mabel.
They were close as sisters and in age
—although Mabel never told
anyone her exact birth date.

At family picnics Mabel played
the mouth-organ, while May sang
in Russian. They both would sing
"The Red River Valley" in English,
with everyone joining in.

Auntie May knew the traditional
a cappella Doukhobor hymns;
she once sang these for a broadcast.

In her 80s, Auntie May rode
a Greyhound bus all the way
to San Diego; she wanted to visit
her son and grandsons living there.

When she came home she said,
"Everyone on the bus ride
was real good to me."

Mabel, always smartly dressed,
was twice married and widowed.
In the later years of her life
a younger man loved her dearly;
he bought them a condo
and devoted himself to her,
taking part at all the family picnics.

Auntie May was living on her own
when we celebrated her ninetieth
birthday—she was the oldest one
still alive from when the Doukhobors
had first imigrated to Canada.

But when both May and Mabel reached
their nineties, they lived together
in a nursing home. By then, Mabel
could not walk—she who had always
loved to dress up and liven every party
with music and dancing. Auntie May
was still active, until very near the end.

May and Mabel died within a few short
weeks of each other—May, as always,
leading the way, passed first at age 94.

Throughout my life I remember these
two great-aunts, both less than five feet
tall, but filled with abundant love of life.

Whenever I saw Auntie May
or spoke to her on the phone,
she ended every conversation
by telling me how much she loved
me and saying, "God bless you."

LETTING THE WINDS OF CHANGE BLOW FREELY

Dear Reader:

The poet is signing off
for now—these poems
began to clamour
at the threshold
of my psyche in the year
following the millennium.

Since then I've toiled,
applied my craft and art,
shared intimate moments
as best I could. If you find
mistakes, blame me;
if you find inspiration,
thank the poetry. This
is not an advertisement—
it is a salutation to you.

As you go about your daily life
and dream your personal dreams,
I hope the winds of change
blow freely through your soul
and new ideas guide your mind.

Try (and I will too) to keep
opinions to yourself.
Instead, watch the world
and listen closely—learn
what there is of wisdom—
then share deeply with others.

A plastic glow-in-the-dark
Mary and a Buddha
made of cheap pottery
sit together on my bedside
table—although I am
neither Catholic nor Buddhist.

But when I turn the lights
off each night, I say
"goodnight Mary, goodnight
Buddha, goodnight moon"
as in the children's book
where the light fades page by
page, in each successive drawing.

And so, goodnight reader—
may whatever God you believe in
bless you—or without
belief in the Divine,
may the force be with you.

All my love,

    CZ

Acknowledgements

Some of the poems in this present collection have appeared or will appear in the following periodicals, online sites, and anthologies. "My Body is Also a Map" and "Living in Exile" are included in the essay "Foremothers: Four Modernist Women Poets from the West Coast", written for the conference, Wider Boundaries of Daring, University of Windsor, Windsor, Ontario, 2001. The anthology, *Re:Generations: Canadian Women Poets in Conversation*, edited by Di Brandt and Barbara Godard, is published by Black Moss Press, 2005.

The glosa, "Living in Exile", was written in honour of P.K. Page, for the conference, *Extraordinary Presence: The Worlds of P.K. Page*, Trent University, Peterborough, Ontario, 2002. This poem first appeared on the conference website. "My Body is a Machine" appeared on the website for The Cosmic Data-Bank. "Beloved" was first published online at The Fraser Valley Astrological Guild website. "Learning to Float" (part one, two) and "Dead Man's Float" (part one, two and three) appear in Issue #2 of *Mad Hatter's Review*, New York City, NY.

"Name Change" was translated into French by Elizabeth Robert and appears in Issue #63 of the feminist periodical *Arcade*, Montreal, Quebec, Summer 2005. *Seed-Time: A Sonnet Sequence* is a limited edition chapbook, Coracle Press, Montreal, Quebec, 2005.

About the Author

Carolyn Zonailo was born in Vancouver, Canada and has lived for the past fifteen years in Montreal. She has published ten previous books of poetry, several chapbooks and one book of prose poems. Her work has appeared in periodicals and anthologies since the mid-1970s. In a poetic voice that is intimate and immediate, Carolyn Zonailo shares her personal experiences, from where she lives in time and place. She draws on her Doukhobor (spirit wrestler) heritage to create poems that are at once earthy and grounded in the everyday, yet at the same time luminous and spiritual. Zonailo's lyrical poetry and long poems have been set to music by different musicians and composers. They have been performed live and recorded, most recently on a new CD by Kate Hammett-Vaughn, Fall 2005, Vancouver, B.C.

Zonailo has an M.A. in literature from Simon Fraser University, where her papers are now archived in Special Collections and Rare Books at the W.A.C. Bennett Library. She has taught creative writing; and been active in literary small press publishing, founding Caitlin Press in 1977. Zonailo has served on the executives of provincial and national writing organizations, including The League of Canadian Poets and The Writers' Union of Canada. Her areas of study encompass literature, mythology, Jungian and archetypal psychology, and astrology. She works as a freelance editor and consultant. *The Goddess in the Garden*, Ekstasis Editions 2002, was a finalist for the A.M. Klein Poetry Prize. Visit her website at: www.carolynzonailo.com